NATURE'S CREEPIEST CREATURES

CREEPY SEA CREATURES

By Nicole Shea

Gareth Stevens Publishing

Please visit our website, www.garethstevens.com. For a free color catalog of all our high-quality books, call toll free 1-800-542-2595 or fax 1-877-542-2596.

Library of Congress Cataloging-in-Publication Data

Shea, Nicole, 1976-
Creepy sea creatures / Nicole Shea.
    p. cm. — (Nature's creepiest creatures)
Includes index.
ISBN 978-1-4339-6503-6 (pbk.)
ISBN 978-1-4339-6504-3 (6-pack)
ISBN 978-1-4339-6501-2 (library binding)
1. Marine animals—Juvenile literature. I. Title.
QL122.2.S52 2012
591.77—dc23
                                    2011037100

First Edition

Published in 2012 by
Gareth Stevens Publishing
111 East 14th Street, Suite 349
New York, NY 10003

Copyright © 2012 Gareth Stevens Publishing

Designer: Haley W. Harasymiw
Editor: Kristen Rajczak

Photo credits: Cover, pp. 1, 6, 7, 9, 11, 13, 17, 20 Shutterstock.com; p. 5 David Hall/Getty Images; p. 15 Solvin Zankl/Getty Images; p. 19 Brian J. Skerry/National Geographic/Getty Images.

Printed in the United States of America

CPSIA compliance information: Batch #CW12GS: For further information contact Gareth Stevens, New York, New York at 1-800-542-2595.

CONTENTS

Words in the glossary appear in **bold** type the first time they are used in the text.

IN THE OCEAN

Many sea creatures live so far underwater, they never see sunlight. These deepwater creatures often have such creepy features, you might wish they'd stay down there! But you don't have to look miles below the ocean's surface to find strange sea creatures.

One such creature is the handfish, which lives in shallow waters near Australia. Named for its weirdly shaped fins, the handfish is hard to find. One kind—the pink handfish—has only been spotted four times!

FREAKY FACT:

Handfish use their hand-shaped fins to walk across the ocean floor instead of swimming through the water.

5

STARGAZERS

The stargazer is always looking up, but it's not looking at the stars. Its eyes are on top of its head! This lets the fish hide in the sand on the seafloor and still see what's going on above it.

To bring **prey** closer, some stargazers also have a body part attached to their lower lip that can look like a squirming worm. When an unlucky fish tries to catch the "worm," the stargazer strikes!

FREAKY FACT:
A lot of fish can poison you or give you an electric shock. Some stargazers can do both!

7

A DANGEROUS NAME FOR A PEACEFUL ANIMAL

Leafy sea dragons are cousins of the seahorse. They look like the seaweed they live in. Body parts that look like leaves cover the leafy sea dragon, offering great **camouflage**. They have tiny fins to help them move through the water, but leafy sea dragons more often just drift with the currents.

Leafy sea dragons are unusual parents. The female lays her bright-pink eggs on patches on the male's tail. The male carries the eggs until the tiny sea dragons are ready to **hatch**.

FREAKY FACT:

Leafy sea dragons don't have teeth. They eat by sucking food into their tube-shaped **snouts**.

Hiding in plain sight can be the best trick of all!

BLUE-RINGED OCTOPUS: BEAUTIFUL DANGER

Although the bright blue rings of this tiny octopus are beautiful, their brightness means deadly danger. This small creature uses **venom** to kill its dinner and to **protect** itself.

First, the blue-ringed octopus uses its eight arms to catch the crabs and shrimp it likes to eat. Then, it bites! Venom **paralyzes** the prey. The blue-ringed octopus's venom is more powerful than any land animal's venom. One bite can kill a person in just a few minutes!

FREAKY FACT:

The mother blue-ringed octopus carries her eggs under her arms. Once the babies hatch, the mother dies.

An octopus's blue rings only appear when it's scared or excited.

HIDDEN STONEFISH

Stonefish are the most poisonous fish in the world. Even creepier, they're hard to see! They blend in perfectly with their surroundings. They look just like stones or rocks on the ocean floor.

Hiding works well for stonefish trying to catch prey and hide from enemies. However, they can be dangerous to someone walking or swimming in their shallow-water homes. As many as 13 venomous **spines** line the stonefish's back! Stepping on a stonefish could be deadly.

FREAKY FACT:

The stonefish's spines are so sharp and strong they can even poke through the thin sole of a shoe!

Viperfish only reach a length of about 1 foot (30 cm). However, their clever hunting method makes up for their lack of size.

The viperfish uses a body part called a photophore to draw prey in. It produces a light at the end of a spine and is used like a fishing rod. Curious fish following the light don't stand a chance against the viperfish's long, sharp teeth! This creepy deepwater fish bites just as fast as the snake it's named after.

FREAKY FACT:

A viperfish's stomach can stretch to twice its normal size in order to eat lots of food when it's available.

Viperfish live thousands of feet below the ocean's surface.

PORTUGUESE MAN-OF-WAR

Try not to get hugged by these arms! A Portuguese man-of-war has long **tentacles** that can reach 165 feet (50 m) in length! They hang from a body part called a float, which looks like a gas-filled bubble on top of the water.

The Portuguese man-of-war has three kinds of tentacles. One helps with making babies, one breaks down food, and the other finds and stings prey. What's the weirdest fact about the Portuguese man-of-war? It's not one animal! It's a group of animals called polyps.

FREAKY FACT:

A little fish called the man-of-war fish lives among the Portuguese man-of-war's stinging tentacles without being hurt. It even eats them!

GIANT SQUID

For thousands of years, sailors have told stories about a terrible sea creature with long, terrifying arms that grabs people and sinks ships. Many scientists think these stories are about the shy—but scary-looking—giant squid. It's not hard to guess why!

Giant squids grow to about 33 feet (10 m) long. However, scientists found one that was 59 feet (18 m) long! Giant squids have eight arms. They also have two tentacles that bring the fish and shrimp they eat to their mouth.

FREAKY FACT:

At almost 10 inches (25 cm) wide, the giant squid's eye is one of the largest in the animal world. It's as wide as a basketball!

Scientists don't know a lot about the giant squid. It lives so deep in the ocean that it's hard to study.

WHAT'S FOR DINNER?

Would you eat a sea creature that looks like a giant spider? In Spain and Japan, spider crab is often served for dinner!

Spider crabs like to hide. They make their homes at the edge of the ocean in tall sea grasses or among rocks. They mostly come out at night. Spider crabs have prickly hairs all over their body. The crabs stick seaweed and sponges on their shells in order to look more like their surroundings.

FREAKY FACT:

A fisherman caught a Japanese spider crab that had a body the size of a soccer ball!

RECORD-BREAKING SEA CREATURES

RECORD	SEA CREATURE
deepest home	Snailfish have been found 4.8 miles (7.7 km) below the ocean's surface.
largest	The blue whale can grow to be 100 feet (30 m) long.
fastest	Fisherman and scientists have reported that sailfish can swim 68 to 75 miles (110 to 120 km) per hour.
deadliest	The sting of a box jellyfish can kill a person in minutes.
oldest alive	Some deep-sea coral dates back 4,265 years.

GLOSSARY

camouflage: something that helps an animal hide itself by looking like its surroundings

hatch: to break out of an egg

paralyze: to prevent something from moving

prey: an animal that is hunted by other animals for food

protect: to keep safe

snout: an animal's nose and mouth

spine: one of many stiff, pointed parts growing from an animal

tentacle: a long, bendable body part that can be used to hold things

venom: poisonous matter created by an animal and passed on by a bite or sting

FOR MORE INFORMATION

Books

Lynette, Rachel. *Deep-Sea Anglerfish and Other Fearsome Fish.* Chicago, IL: Raintree Publishing, 2012.

Stierle, Cynthia. *Ocean Life from A to Z.* Pleasantville, NY: Reader's Digest Children's Books, 2007.

Websites

Earth's Kids: Oceans and Marine Life Science
www.earthskids.com/ek_science-marine.htm
Learn more about life in the ocean.

Nat Geo Wild: Fish
animals.nationalgeographic.com/animals/fish/
Look at pictures, watch videos, and read about fish from all over the world.

INDEX